D1607264

DARREN CRISS

By Amy Davidson

Gareth Stevens
Publishing

RIGHT ON!

Please visit our website, www.garethstevens.com. For a free color catalog of all our
high-quality books, call toll free 1-800-542-2595 or fax 1-877-542-2596.

Library of Congress Cataloging-in-Publication Data

Davidson, Amy, 1988-
 Darren Criss / Amy Davidson.
    p. cm. — (Rising stars)
 Includes index.
ISBN 978-1-4339-7277-5 (pbk.)
ISBN 978-1-4339-7278-2 (6-pack)
ISBN 978-1-4339-7276-8 (library binding)
1. Criss, Darren—Juvenile literature. 2. Actors—United States—Biography—Juvenile litera-
ture. 3. Singers—United States—Biography—Juvenile literature. I. Title.
 PN2287.C6715D38 2013
 792.02'8092—dc23
 [B]
                                2012007831

First Edition

Published in 2013 by Gareth Stevens Publishing
111 East 14th Street, Suite 349
New York, NY 10003

Designer: Ben Gardner
Editor: Katie Kawa

Photo credits: Cover background Shutterstock.com; cover, pp. 1, 5 Fanzer Harrison/
Getty Images; p. 7 Rob Kim/Getty Imges; pp. 9, 23 Mike Coppola/Getty Images;
p. 11 Stephen Lovekin/Getty Images; p. 13 Charley Gallay/Getty Images; p. 15 Sam Aronov/
Shutterstock.com; p. 17 DFree/Shutterstock.com; p. 19 Michael Buckner/AMA2010/
Getty Images Entertainment/Getty Images; p. 21 Kevin Winter/Getty Images;
pp. 25, 29 Featureflash/Shutterstock.com; p. 27 Bruce Glikas/Getty Images.

Printed in the United States of America

CPSIA compliance information: Batch #CS12GS: For further information contact Gareth Stevens, New York, New York at 1-800-542-2595.

Contents

Meet Darren

Darren Criss is an actor and a singer.

He has fans all over the world!

5

Darren was born on February 5, 1987.

He grew up in San Francisco,

California. Darren always loved

making music!

Making Music

Darren plays many musical instruments.
Some of the instruments he plays are
piano, guitar, violin, and drums.

Fun at School

Darren studied acting in college. He went to a school called the University of Michigan. He finished college in 2009.

THE HUN[...]
BEGIN[...]

11

Darren wrote and acted in plays with
his friends from college. They called
themselves Team StarKid. They put
their plays on YouTube. They were
a huge hit!

In 2009, Darren and his friends wrote a play about the Harry Potter books called *A Very Potter Musical*. Darren played Harry Potter. The play has been viewed more than 3 million times on YouTube!

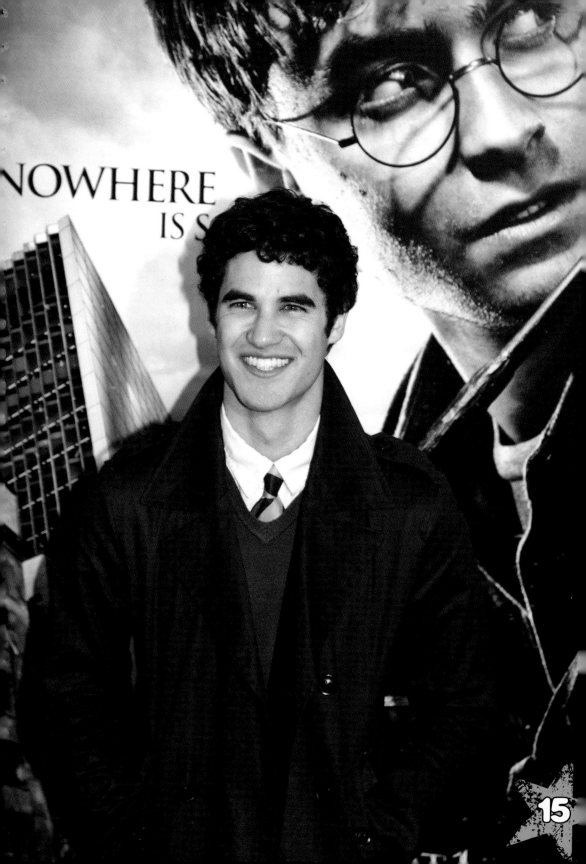

NOWHERE
IS S

15

A Hit Show

In 2010, Darren started playing Blaine Anderson on the TV show *Glee*. He has sung many popular songs on the show. It made him a star!

The first song Darren sang on *Glee*
was "Teenage Dream" by Katy Perry.
It was the first song from *Glee* to
reach number 1 on the Billboard
Hot 100 chart.

Katy Perry

19

Darren has won awards for playing Blaine.

In 2011, he won a Teen Choice Award for

Choice TV Breakout Star.

On Tour

In the summer of 2011, Darren went on tour with the rest of the *Glee* cast. They sang songs from the show in front of thousands of fans!

A movie about the tour came out in 2011, too. It was called *Glee: The 3D Concert Movie*. Fans got to see Darren in a movie for the first time!

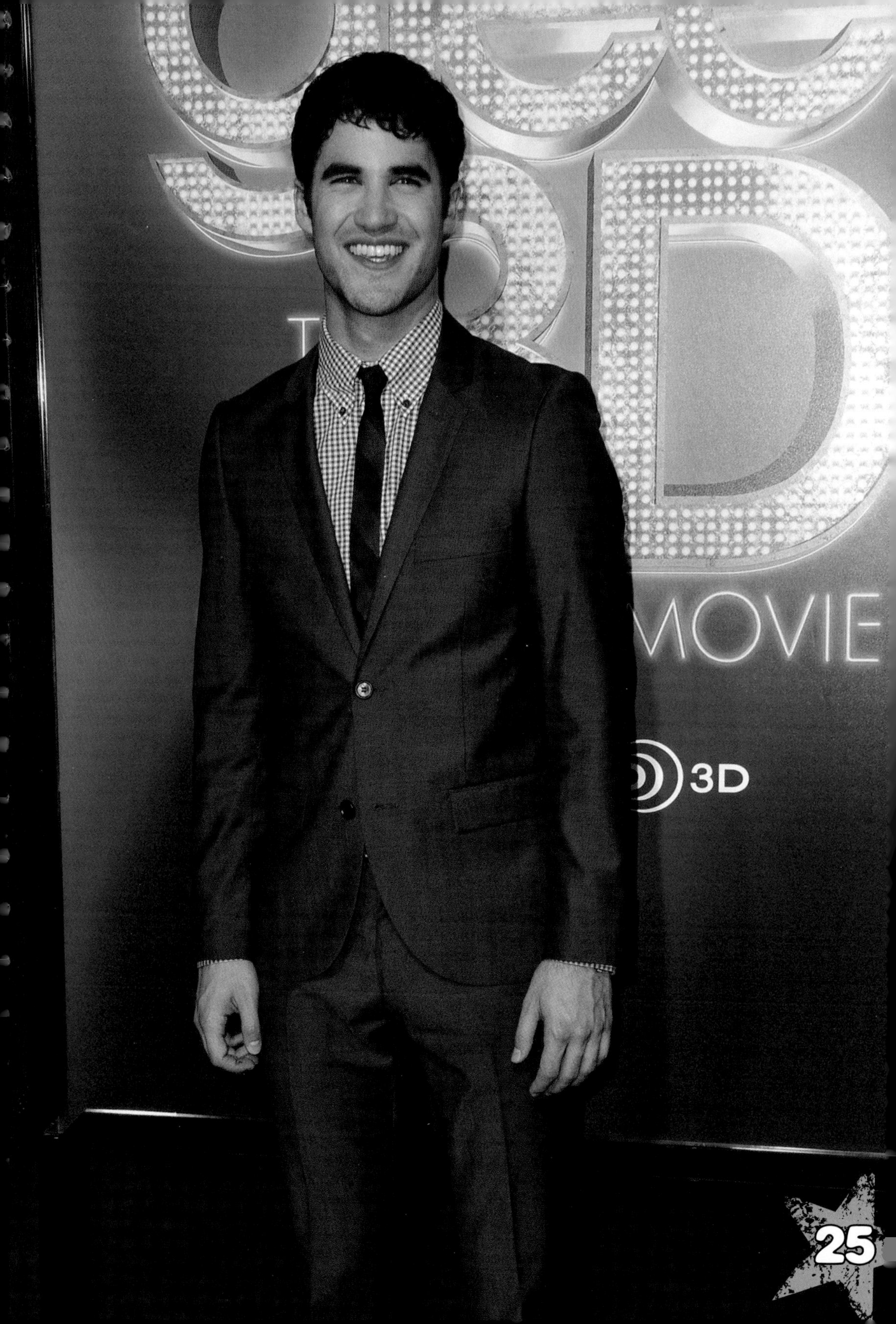
MOVIE
3D

On the Stage

In 2012, Darren starred on Broadway in *How to Succeed in Business Without Really Trying*. He played J. Pierrepont Finch in this famous play. Many of Darren's fans came to see him.

What's Next?

Darren has worked hard to become a star. What will he do next?

Timeline

1987   Darren is born on February 5.

2009   Darren plays Harry Potter in *A Very Potter Musical.*

          Darren graduates from the University of Michigan.

2010   Darren starts playing Blaine Anderson on *Glee.*

2011   Darren wins Teen Choice Award for Choice TV Breakout Star.

          Darren goes on tour with the *Glee* cast.

          Glee: The 3D Concert Movie comes out in August.

2012   Darren stars in *How to Succeed in Business Without Really Trying.*

For More Information

Books

Rickman, Amy. *Gleeful! A Totally Unofficial Guide to the Hit TV Series* Glee. New York, NY: Villard Trade Paperbacks, 2010.

Websites

Darren Criss

darrencriss.snappages.com

Keep up with the latest news about Darren's career, and watch videos of him performing.

Darren Criss Web

darrencrissweb.com

Find out more about Darren's work as an actor and a musician.

Glee

www.fox.com/glee

Watch videos and learn more about the TV show that made Darren a star.

Glossary

award: a prize given for doing something well

college: a school after high school

instrument: something that is used to make music

million: the number that is equal to a thousand thousands; 1,000,000

tour: when a person or group travels to different places to sing

Index